Chamber Music
and Other Poems

Chamber Music

and Other Poems

James Joyce

ALMA CLASSICS

ALMA CLASSICS
an imprint of

ALMA BOOKS LTD
3 Castle Yard
Richmond
Surrey TW10 6TF
United Kingdom
www.almaclassics.com

Chamber Music first published in 1907
Pomes Penyeach first published in 1927
This collection first published by Alma Classics in 2017

Extra Material © Alma Books Ltd

Printed in Great Britain by CPI Group (UK) Ltd, Croydon CR0 4YY

ISBN: 978-1-84749-585-3

Contents

CHAMBER MUSIC*

(1907)

I

Strings in the earth and air
   Make music sweet;
Strings by the river where
   The willows meet.

There's music along the river
   For Love wanders there,
Pale flowers on his mantle
   Dark leaves on his hair.

All softly playing,
   With head to the music bent,
And fingers straying
   Upon an instrument.

II

The twilight turns from amethyst
    To deep and deeper blue,
The lamp fills with a pale-green glow
    The trees of the avenue.

The old piano plays an air,
    Sedate and slow and gay;
She bends upon the yellow keys,
    Her head inclines this way.

Shy thoughts and grave wide eyes and hands
    That wander as they list –
The twilight turns to darker blue
    With lights of amethyst.

III

At that hour when all things have repose,
  O lonely watcher of the skies,
  Do you hear the night wind and the sighs
Of harps playing unto Love to unclose
  The pale gates of sunrise?

When all things repose do you alone
  Awake to hear the sweet harps play
  To Love before him on his way,
And the night wind answering in antiphon
  Till night is overgone?

Play on, invisible harps, unto Love
  Whose way in heaven is aglow
  At that hour when soft lights come and go,
Soft sweet music in the air above
  And in the earth below.

IV

When the shy star goes forth in heaven
   All maidenly, disconsolate,
Hear you amid the drowsy even
   One who is singing by your gate.
His song is softer than the dew
   And he is come to visit you.

Oh bend no more in reverie
   When he at eventide is calling
Nor muse: Who may this singer be
   Whose song about my heart is falling?
Know you by this, the lover's chant,
   'Tis I that am your visitant.

V

Lean out of the window,
  Goldenhair,
I heard you singing
  A merry air.

My book is closed;
  I read no more,
Watching the fire dance
  On the floor.

I have left my book:
  I have left my room:
For I heard you singing
  Through the gloom,

Singing and singing
  A merry air.
Lean out of the window,
  Goldenhair.

VI

I would in that sweet bosom be
   (Oh sweet it is and fair it is!)
Where no rude wind might visit me.
   Because of sad austerities
I would in that sweet bosom be.

I would be ever in that heart
   (Oh soft I knock and soft entreat her!)
Where only peace might be my part.
   Austerities were all the sweeter
So I were ever in that heart.

VII

My love is in a light attire
  Among the apple trees
Where the gay winds do most desire
  To run in companies.

There, where the gay winds stay to woo
  The young leaves as they pass,
My love goes slowly, bending to
  Her shadow on the grass;

And where the sky's a pale-blue cup
  Over the laughing land,
My love goes lightly, holding up
  Her dress with dainty hand.

VIII

Who goes amid the green wood
  With spring tide all adorning her?
Who goes amid the merry green wood
  To make it merrier?

Who passes in the sunlight
  By ways that know the light footfall?
Who passes in the sweet sunlight
  With mien so virginal?

The ways of all the woodland
  Gleam with a soft and golden fire –
For whom does all the sunny woodland
  Carry so brave attire?

Oh, it is for my true love
  The woods their rich apparel wear –
Oh, it is for my own true love,
  That is so young and fair.

IX

Winds of May, that dance on the sea,
  Dancing a ring-around in glee
From furrow to furrow, while overhead
The foam flies up to be garlanded
In silvery arches spanning the air,
Saw you my true love anywhere?
       Welladay! Welladay!
      For the winds of May!
  Love is unhappy when love is away!

X

Bright cap and streamers,
   He sings in the hollow:
   Come follow, come follow,
      All you that love.
Leave dreams to the dreamers
   That will not after,
   That song and laughter
      Do nothing move.

With ribbons streaming
   He sings the bolder;
   In troop at his shoulder
      The wild bees hum.
And the time of dreaming
   Dreams is over –
   As lover to lover,
      Sweetheart, I come.

XI

Bid adieu, adieu, adieu,
   Bid adieu to girlish days.
Happy Love is come to woo
   Thee and woo thy girlish ways –
The zone that doth become thee fair,
The snood upon thy yellow hair,

When thou hast heard his name upon
   The bugles of the cherubim
Begin thou softly to unzone
   Thy girlish bosom unto him
And softly to undo the snood
That is the sign of maidenhood.

XII

What counsel has the hooded moon
  Put in thy heart, my shyly sweet,
Of Love in ancient plenilune,
  Glory and stars beneath his feet –
A sage that is but kith and kin
With the comedian capuchin?

Believe me rather that am wise
  In disregard of the divine.
A glory kindles in those eyes,
  Trembles to starlight. Mine, O mine!
No more be tears in moon or mist
For thee, sweet sentimentalist.

XIII

Go seek her out all courteously
   And say I come,
Wind of spices whose song is ever
   Epithalamium.
Oh, hurry over the dark lands
   And run upon the sea
For seas and lands shall not divide us,
   My love and me.

Now, wind, of your good courtesy
   I pray you go
And come into her little garden
   And sing at her window;
Singing: The bridal wind is blowing
   For Love is at his noon;
And soon will your true love be with you,
   Soon, oh soon.

XIV

My dove, my beautiful one,
   Arise, arise!
   The night dew lies
Upon my lips and eyes.

The odorous winds are weaving
   A music of sighs:
   Arise, arise,
My dove, my beautiful one!

I wait by the cedar tree,
   My sister, my love.
   White breast of the dove,
My breast shall be your bed.

The pale dew lies
Like a veil on my head.
   My fair one, my fair dove,
Arise, arise!

XV

From dewy dreams, my soul, arise,
  From love's deep slumber and from death,
For lo! the trees are full of sighs
  Whose leaves the morn admonisheth.

Eastward the gradual dawn prevails
  Where softly burning fires appear,
Making to tremble all those veils
  Of grey and golden gossamer.

While sweetly, gently, secretly,
  The flowery bells of morn are stirred
And the wise choirs of faery
  Begin (innumerous!) to be heard.

XVI

Oh cool is the valley now
  And there, love, will we go
For many a choir is singing now
  Where Love did some time go.
And hear you not the thrushes calling,
  Calling us away?
Oh cool and pleasant is the valley
  And there, love, will we stay.

XVII

Because your voice was at my side
　　I gave him pain,
Because within my hand I had
　　Your hand again.

There is no word nor any sign
　　Can make amend –
He is a stranger to me now
　　Who was my friend.

XVIII

O sweetheart, hear you
   Your lover's tale;
A man shall have sorrow
   When friends him fail.

For he shall know then
   Friends be untrue
And a little ashes
   Their words come to.

But one unto him
   Will softly move
And softly woo him
   In ways of love.

His hand is under
   Her smooth round breast;
So he who has sorrow
   Shall have rest.

XIX

Be not sad because all men
   Prefer a lying clamour before you:
Sweetheart, be at peace again –
   Can they dishonour you?

They are sadder than all tears;
   Their lives ascend as a continual sigh.
Proudly answer to their tears:
   As they deny, deny.

XX

In the dark pinewood
   I would we lay,
In deep cool shadow
    At noon of day.

How sweet to lie there,
    Sweet to kiss,
Where the great pine forest
    Enaisled is!

Thy kiss descending
    Sweeter were
With a soft tumult
    Of thy hair.

Oh, unto the pinewood
    At noon of day
Come with me now,
    Sweet love, away.

XXI

He who hath glory lost nor hath
   Found any soul to fellow his,
Among his foes in scorn and wrath
   Holding to ancient nobleness,
That high unconsortable one –
His love is his companion.

XXII

Of that so sweet imprisonment
   My soul, dearest, is fain –
Soft arms that woo me to relent
   And woo me to detain.
Ah, could they ever hold me there,
Gladly were I a prisoner!

Dearest, through interwoven arms
   By love made tremulous,
That night allures me where alarms
   Nowise may trouble us
But sleep to dreamier sleep be wed
Where soul with soul lies prisoned.

XXIII

This heart that flutters near my heart
    My hope and all my riches is,
Unhappy when we draw apart
    And happy between kiss and kiss;
My hope and all my riches – yes! –
And all my happiness.

For there, as in some mossy nest
    The wrens will divers treasures keep,
I laid those treasures I possessed
    Ere that mine eyes had learned to weep.
Shall we not be as wise as they
Though love live but a day?

XXIV

Silently she's combing,
　　Combing her long hair,
Silently and graciously,
　　With many a pretty air.

The sun is in the willow leaves
　　And on the dappled grass
And still she's combing her long hair
　　Before the looking glass.

I pray you, cease to comb out,
　　Comb out your long hair,
For I have heard of witchery
　　Under a pretty air,

That makes as one thing to the lover
　　Staying and going hence,
All fair, with many a pretty air
　　And many a negligence.

XXV

Lightly come or lightly go
   Though thy heart presage thee woe,
Vales and many a wasted sun,
   Oread* let thy laughter run
Till the irreverent mountain air
Ripple all thy flying hair.

Lightly, lightly – ever so:
   Clouds that wrap the vales below
At the hour of even-star
   Lowliest attendants are:
Love and laughter song-confessed
When the heart is heaviest.

XXVI

Thou leanest to the shell of night,
　　Dear lady, a divining ear.
In that soft choiring of delight
　　What sound hath made thy heart to fear?
Seemed it of rivers rushing forth
From the grey deserts of the north?

That mood of thine, O timorous,
　　Is his, if thou but scan it well,
Who a mad tale bequeaths to us
　　At ghosting hour conjurable –
And all for some strange name he read
In Purchas or in Holinshed.*

XXVII

Though I thy Mithridates* were
  Framed to defy the poison dart,
Yet must thou fold me unaware
  To know the rapture of thy heart
And I but render and confess
The malice of thy tenderness.

For elegant and antique phrase,
  Dearest, my lips wax all too wise;
Nor have I known a love whose praise
  Our piping poets solemnize,
Neither a love where may not be
Ever so little falsity.

XXVIII

Gentle lady, do not sing
   Sad songs about the end of love;
Lay aside sadness and sing
   How love that passes is enough.

Sing about the long deep sleep
   Of lovers that are dead and how
In the grave all love shall sleep.
   Love is aweary now.

XXIX

Dear heart, why will you use me so?
   Dear eyes that gently me upbraid
Still are you beautiful – but oh,
   How is your beauty raimented!

Through the clear mirror of your eyes,
   Through the soft sigh of kiss to kiss,
Desolate winds assail with cries
   The shadowy garden where love is.

And soon shall love dissolved be
   When over us the wild winds blow –
But you, dear love, too dear to me,
   Alas! why will you use me so?

XXX

Love came to us in time gone by
   When one at twilight shyly played
And one in fear was standing nigh –
   For Love at first is all afraid.

We were grave lovers. Love is past
   That had his sweet hours many a one.
Welcome to us now at the last
   The ways that we shall go upon.

XXXI

Oh, it was out by Donnycarney*
  When the bat flew from tree to tree
My love and I did walk together
  And sweet were the words she said to me.

Along with us the summer wind
  Went murmuring – oh, happily! –
But softer than the breath of summer
  Was the kiss she gave to me.

XXXII

Rain has fallen all the day
 Oh come among the laden trees.
The leaves lie thick upon the way
 Of memories.

Staying a little by the way
 Of memories shall we depart.
Come, my beloved, where I may
 Speak to your heart.

XXXIII

Now, oh now, in this brown land
   Where Love did so sweet music make
We two shall wander, hand in hand,
   Forbearing for old friendship's sake
Nor grieve because our love was gay
Which now is ended in this way.

A rogue in red-and-yellow dress
   Is knocking, knocking at the tree
And all around our loneliness
   The wind is whistling merrily.
The leaves – they do not sigh at all
When the year takes them in the fall.

Now, oh now, we hear no more
   The villanelle and roundelay!
Yet will we kiss, sweetheart, before
   We take sad leave at close of day.
Grieve not, sweetheart, for anything –
The year, the year is gathering.

XXXIV

Sleep now, oh sleep now,
   O you unquiet heart!
A voice crying "Sleep now"
   Is heard in my heart.

The voice of the winter
   Is heard at the door.
Oh sleep for the winter
   Is crying "Sleep no more!"

My kiss will give peace now
   And quiet to your heart –
Sleep on in peace now,
   O you unquiet heart!

XXXV

All day I hear the noise of waters
    Making moan
Sad as the seabird is when going
    Forth alone
He hears the winds cry to the waters'
    Monotone.

The grey winds, the cold winds are blowing
    Where I go.
I hear the noise of many waters
    Far below.
All day, all night, I hear them flowing
    To and fro.

XXXVI

I hear an army charging upon the land
    And the thunder of horses plunging, foam about their knees.
Arrogant, in black armour, behind them stand,
    Disdaining the reins, with fluttering whips, the charioteers.

They cry unto the night their battle name:
    I moan in sleep when I hear afar their whirling laughter.
They cleave the gloom of dreams, a blinding flame,
    Clanging, clanging upon the heart as upon an anvil.

They come shaking in triumph their long green hair:
    They come out of the sea and run shouting by the shore.
My heart, have you no wisdom thus to despair?
    My love, my love, my love, why have you left me alone?

POMES PENYEACH*

(1927)

Tilly

He travels after a winter sun,
Urging the cattle along a cold red road,
Calling to them, a voice they know,
He drives his beasts above Cabra.*

The voice tells them home is warm.
They moo and make brute music with their hoofs.
He drives them with a flowering branch before him,
Smoke pluming their foreheads.

Boor, bond of the herd,
Tonight stretch full by the fire!
I bleed by the black stream
For my torn bough!

Dublin, 1904

Watching the
Needleboats at San Sabba*

I heard their young hearts crying
Loveward above the glancing oar
And heard the prairie grasses sighing:
No more, return no more! *

O hearts, O sighing grasses,
Vainly your love-blown bannerets mourn!
No more will the wild wind that passes
Return, no more return.

Trieste, 1912

A Flower Given to My Daughter

Frail the white rose and frail are
Her hands that gave
Whose soul is sere and paler
Than time's wan wave.

Rose-frail and fair – yet frailest
A wonder wild
In gentle eyes thou veilest,
My blue-veined child.

Trieste, 1913

She Weeps over Rahoon*

Rain on Rahoon falls softly, softly falling,
Where my dark lover lies.
Sad is his voice that calls me, sadly calling,
At grey moonrise.

Love, hear thou
How soft, how sad his voice is ever calling,
Ever unanswered, and the dark rain falling,
Then as now.

Dark too our hearts, O love, shall lie and cold
As his sad heart has lain
Under the moon-grey nettles, the black mould
And muttering rain.

Trieste, 1913

Tutto è sciolto*

A birdless heaven, seadusk, one lone star
Piercing the west,
As thou, fond heart, love's time, so faint, so far,
Rememberest.

The clear young eyes' soft look, the candid brow,
The fragrant hair,
Falling as through the silence falleth now
Dusk of the air.

Why then, remembering those shy
Sweet lures, repine
When the dear love she yielded with a sigh
Was all but thine?

Trieste, 1914

On the Beach at Fontana*

Wind whines and whines the shingle,
The crazy pier stakes groan;
A senile sea numbers each single
Slime-silvered stone.

From whining wind and colder
Grey sea I wrap him warm
And touch his trembling fine-boned shoulder
And boyish arm.

Around us fear, descending
Darkness of fear above
And in my heart how deep unending
Ache of love!

Trieste, 1914

Simples

O bella bionda,
sei come l'onda!*

Of cool sweet dew and radiance mild
The moon a web of silence weaves
In the still garden where a child
Gathers the simple salad leaves.

A moon-dew stars her hanging hair
And moonlight kisses her young brow
And, gathering, she sings an air:
Fair as the wave is, fair, art thou!

Be mine, I pray, a waxen ear
To shield me from her childish croon
And mine a shielded heart for her
Who gathers simples of the moon.

Trieste, 1915

Flood

Gold-brown upon the sated flood
The rock-vine clusters lift and sway;
Vast wings above the lambent waters brood
Of sullen day.

A waste of waters ruthlessly
Sways and uplifts its weedy mane
Where brooding day stares down upon the sea
In dull disdain.

Uplift and sway, O golden vine,
Your clustered fruits to love's full flood,
Lambent and vast and ruthless as is thine
Incertitude!

Trieste, 1915

Nightpiece

Gaunt in gloom,
The pale stars their torches,
Enshrouded, wave.
Ghost fires from heaven's far verges faint illume,
Arches on soaring arches,
Night's sin-dark nave.

Seraphim,
The lost hosts awaken
To service till
In moonless gloom each lapses muted, dim,
Raised when she has and shaken
Her thurible.

And long and loud,
To night's nave upsoaring,
A star knell tolls
As the bleak incense surges, cloud on cloud,
Voidward from the adoring
Waste of souls.

Trieste, 1915

Alone

The moon's grey-golden meshes make
All night a veil,
The shore lamps in the sleeping lake
Laburnum tendrils trail.

The sly reeds whisper to the night
A name – her name –
And all my soul is a delight,
A swoon of shame.

Zurich, 1916

A Memory of the Players
in a Mirror at Midnight

They mouth love's language. Gnash
The thirteen teeth
Your lean jaws grin with. Lash
Your itch and quailing, nude greed of the flesh.
Love's breath in you is stale, worded or sung,
As sour as cat's breath,
Harsh of tongue.

This grey that stares
Lies not, stark skin and bone.
Leave greasy lips their kissing. None
Will choose her what you see to mouth upon.
Dire hunger holds his hour.
Pluck forth your heart, salt-blood, a fruit of tears.
Pluck and devour!

Zurich, 1917

Bahnhofstrasse*

The eyes that mock me sign the way
Whereto I pass at eve of day,

Grey way whose violet signals are
The trysting and the twining star.

Ah star of evil! star of pain!
High-hearted youth comes not again

Nor old heart's wisdom yet to know
The signs that mock me as I go.

Zurich, 1918

A Prayer

Again!
Come, give, yield all your strength to me!
From far a low word breathes on the breaking brain
Its cruel calm, submission's misery,
Gentling her awe as to a soul predestined.
Cease, silent love! My doom!

Blind me with your dark nearness, oh have mercy,
      beloved enemy of my will!
I dare not withstand the cold touch that I dread.
Draw from me still
My slow life! Bend deeper on me, threatening head,
Proud by my downfall, remembering, pitying
Him who is, him who was!

Again!
Together, folded by the night, they lay on earth. I hear
From far her low word breathe on my breaking brain.
Come! I yield. Bend deeper upon me! I am here.
Subduer, do not leave me! Only joy, only anguish,
Take me, save me, soothe me, oh spare me!

Paris, 1924

A SELECTION OF
UNCOLLECTED POEMS

Satire on George O'Donnell*

(in the style of Goldsmith)*

Poor little Georgie, the son of a lackey,
Famous for "murphies," spirits, and 'baccy,*
Renowned all around for a feathery head
Which had a tendency to become red.
His genius was such that all men used to stare,
His appearance was that of a bull at a fair.
The pride of Kilmainham,* the joy of the class,
A moony, a loony, an idiot, an ass.
Drumcondra's production,* and by the same rule,
The prince of all pot-boys, a regular fool.
All hail to the beauteous, the lovely, all hail
And hail to his residence in Portland jail.*

(1896–97)

Translation of Horace's
'O fons Bandusiæ'*

Brighter than glass Bandusian spring
   For mellow wine and flowers meet,
The morrow thee a kid shall bring
   Boding of rivalry and sweet
Love in his swelling forms. In vain
He, wanton offspring, deep shall stain
Thy clear cold streams with crimson rain.

The raging dog star's season thou,
   Still safe from in the heat of day,
When oxen weary of the plough
   Yieldst thankful cool for herds that stray.
Be of the noble founts! I sing
The oak tree o'er thine echoing
Crags, thy waters murmuring.

(1898)

Translation of Verlaine's
'Chanson d'automne'*

A voice that sings
Like viol strings
　　Through the wane
Of the pale year
Lulleth me here
　　With its strain.

My soul is faint
At the bell's plaint
　　Ringing deep;
I think upon
A day bygone
　　And I weep.

Away! Away!
I must obey
　　This drear wind,
Like a dead leaf
In aimless grief
　　Drifting blind.

(1900–2)

On Rudolf Goldschmidt*

(to the tune of the 'Amorous Goldfish')*

A Goldschmidt swam in a *Kriegsverein**
As wise little Goldschmidts do,
And he loved every scion of the Habsburg line,
Each Archduke proud, the whole jimbang crowd,
And he felt that they loved him, too.
Herr Rosenbaum and Rosenfeld
And every other Feld except *Schlachtfeld**
All worked like niggers, totting rows of crazy figures,
To save Kaiser Karl and Goldschmidt, too.

CHORUS:
For he said it is bet – bet – better
To stick stamps on some God-damned letter
Than be shot in a trench
Amid shells and stench,
*Jesus Gott, Donnerwet – wet – wetter.**

(November 1917?)

Fragment on Miss Moschos*

Little Miss Moschos
Soft as a mouse goes

(1920s?)

Hue's Hue? or Dalton's Dilemma*

What colour's Jew Joyce when he's rude and grim both,
Varied virid from groening* and rufous with rage
And if this allrotter's allred as a roth*
Can he still blush unirish yet green as a gage?*

(c.1928)

Epigram on the Lady Friends of St James*

As I was going to Joyce Saint James'
I met with seven extravagant dames;
Every dame had a bee in her bonnet,
With bats from the belfry roosting upon it.
And Ah, I said, poor Joyce Saint James,
What can he do with these terrible dames?
Poor Saint James Joyce.

(January 1931)

Pour la rîme seulement*

À Pierre de Lanux
dit Valéry Larbaud,
Prête-moi un dux
qui peut conduire l'assaut.
Mes pioupions* sont fondus*
et meurent de malaise.*
Sois ton petit tondu*
pour la gloire d'Arès.

Lanux de la Pierre
à Beaulard fit réplique,
Fous-moi la guerre
avec tes soldiqués.*
Car pour l'Italie
presto fais tes malles,
tire ta bonne partie
avec quelques balles.

À ces mots Leryval
file en obobus,*
et comme le vieux Hannibal
perce le blocus,
à peine atterre sa mine
qu'on crie à la foire,
un sous la Mursoline*
pour l'arrats* de gloire.

(May 1932)

Epilogue to Ibsen's *Ghosts**

Dear quick, whose conscience buried deep
The grim old grouser* has been salving,
Permit one spectre more to peep.
I am the ghost of Captain Alving.

Silenced and smothered by my past
Like the lewd knight* in dirty linen
I struggle forth to swell the cast
And air a long-suppressed opinion.

For muddling weddings into wakes
No fool could vie with Parson Manders.
I, though a dab at ducks and drakes,
Let gooseys serve or sauce their ganders.

My spouse bore me a blighted boy,
Our slavey pupped a bouncing bitch.
Paternity, thy name is joy
When the wise child knows which is which.

Both swear I am that selfsame man
By whom their infants were begotten.
Explain, fate, if you care and can
Why one is sound and one is rotten.

Olaf may plod his stony path
And live as chastely as Susanna
Yet pick up in some Turkish bath
His *quantum sat* of *Pox Romana.**

While Haakon hikes up primrose way,
Spreeing and gleeing as he goes,
To smirk upon his latter day
Without a pimple on his nose.

I gave it up I am afraid
But if I loafed and found it fun
Remember how a coy-clad maid
Knows how to take it out of one.

The more I dither on and drink
My midnight bowl of spirit punch
The firmlier I feel and think
Friend Manders came too oft to lunch.

Since scuttling ship Vikings like me
Reck not to whom the blame is laid;
YMCA, VD, TB*
Or Harbourmaster of Port Said.

Blame all and none and take to task
The harlot's lure, the swain's desire.
Heal by all means but hardly ask
Did this man sin or did his sire.

The shack's ablaze. That canting scamp,
The carpenter, has dished the parson.
Now had they kept their powder damp
Like me there would have been no arson.

Nay more, were I not all I was,
Weak, wanton, waster out and out,
There would have been no world's applause
And damn all to write home about.

(April 1934)

Translation from Gottfried Keller's
*Lebendig begraben** Suite

Now have I fed and eaten up the rose
Which then she laid within my stiff-cold hand.
That I should ever feed upon a rose
I never had believed in live man's land.

Only I wonder was it white or red
The flower that in this dark my food has been.
Give us, and if Thou give, thy daily bread,
Deliver us from evil, Lord. Amen.

(after April 1934)

A Come-All-Ye,
by a Thanksgiving Turkey

Come all you lairds and lassies and listen to my lay!
I'll tell you of my adventures upon last Thanksgiving Day
I was picked by Madame Jolas* to adorn her barbecue
So the chicken-choker patched me till I looked as good as new.

I drove out, all tarred and feathered, from the Grand Palais Potin*
But I met with foul disaster in the Place Saint-Augustin.
My charioteer collided – with the shock I did explode
And the force of my emotions shot my liver on the road.

Up steps a dapper sergeant with his pencil and his book.
Our names and our convictions down in Lieber's code* he took.
Then I hailed another driver and resumed my swanee way.*
They couldn't find my liver but I hadn't time to stay.

When we reached the gates of Paris cries the boss at the *Octroi*:*
Holy Poule,* what's this I'm seeing? Can it be Grandmother Loye?*
When Caesar got the bird she was the dindy of the flock
But she must have boxed a round or two with some old turkey cock.

I ruffled up my plumage and proclaimed with eagle's pride:
You jackdaw, these are truffles and not blues on my backside.
Mind, said he, that one's a chestnut. There's my bill and here's my thanks
And now please search through your stuffing and fork out that fifty francs.

68

At last I reached the banquet hall – and what a sight to see!
I felt myself transported back among the Osmanli.*
I poured myself a bubbly flask and raised the golden horn
With three cheers for good old Turkey and the roost where I was
     born.

I shook claws with all the hommes* and bowed to blonde and
     brune
The mistress made a signal and the mujik* called the tune.
Madamina* read a message from the Big Noise* of her State
After which we crowed in unison: That Turco's talking straight!*

We settled down to feed and, if you want to know my mind,
I thought that I could gobble but they left me picked behind.
They crammed their chops till cock-shout when like ostriches
     they ran
To hunt my missing liver round the Place Saint-Augustin.

Envoi
Still I'll lift my glass to Gallia and augur that we may
Untroubled in her dovecote dwell till next Thanksgiving Day
So let every Gallic gander pass the sauce-boat to his goose –
And let's all play happy homing though our liver's on the loose.

(November 1937)

John Quinn*

There's a donor of lavish largesse
Who once bought a play in MS.
   He found out what it all meant
   By the final instalment
But poor Scriptor was left in a mess.

(September 1917)

Claude Sykes*

There is a clean climber called Sykes
Who goes scrambling through ditches and dykes.
  To skate on his scalp
  Down the side of an alp
Is the kind of diversion he likes.

(September 1917)

Solomon

(on Simeone Levi)*

There's a hairy-faced Muslim named Simon
Whose tones are not those of a shy man
   When with cast-iron lungs
   He howls twenty-five tongues –
But he's not at all easy to rhyme on.

(September 1917)

D.L.G.*

(on David Lloyd George)

There's a George of the Georges named David
With whose words we are now night and day fed.
  He cries: I'll give small rations
  To all the small nations.
Bully* God made this world – but I'll save it.

(November 1917)

P. J. T.*

(on Patrick Tuohy)

There's a funny face painter dubbed Tuohy
Whose bleak look is rosy-bud bluey
   For when he feels strong
   He feels *your* daub's all wrong
But when he feels weak he feels wooey.

(1925–27)

The Holy Office*

Myself unto myself will give
This name Katharsis-Purgative.*
I, who dishevelled ways forsook
To hold the poets' grammar book,
Bringing to tavern and to brothel
The mind of witty Aristotle,*
Lest bards in the attempt should err
Must here be my interpreter:
Wherefore receive now from my lip
Peripatetic* scholarship.
To enter heaven, travel hell,
Be piteous or terrible
One positively needs the ease
Of plenary indulgences.
For every true-born mysticist
A Dante* is, unprejudiced,
Who safe at ingle-nook, by proxy,
Hazards extremes of heterodoxy,
Like him who finds a joy at table
Pondering the uncomfortable.
Ruling one's life by common sense
How can one fail to be intense?
But I must not accounted be
One of that mumming company* –
With him who hies him to appease*
His giddy dames'* frivolities
While they console him when he whinges
With gold-embroidered Celtic fringes* –

Or him who sober all the day*
Mixes a naggin* in his play –
Or him who conduct "seems to own",
His preference for a man of "tone"* –
Or him who plays the rugged patch
To millionaires in Hazelhatch
But weeping after holy fast
Confesses all his pagan past* –
Or him who will his hat unfix
Neither to malt nor crucifix
But show to all that poor-dressed be
His high Castilian courtesy* –
Or him who loves his Master dear* –
Or him who drinks his pint in fear* –
Or him who once when snug abed
Saw Jesus Christ without his head
And tried so hard to win for us
The long-lost works of Aeschylus.*
But all these men of whom I speak
Make me the sewer of their clique.
That they may dream their dreamy dreams
I carry off their filthy streams
For I can do those things for them
Through which I lost my diadem,
Those things for which Grandmother Church
Left me severely in the lurch.
Thus I relieve their timid arses,
Perform my office of Katharsis.
My scarlet* leaves them white as wool
Through me they purge a bellyful.
To sister mummers one and all
I act as vicar-general*

And for each maiden, shy and nervous,
I do a similar kind service.
For I detect without surprise
That shadowy beauty in her eyes,
The "dare not" of sweet maidenhood
That answers my corruptive "would".
Whenever publicly we meet
She never seems to think of it;
At night when close in bed she lies
And feels my hand between her thighs
My little love in light attire
Knows the soft flame that is desire.
But Mammon* places under ban
The uses of Leviathan*
And that high spirit ever wars
On Mammon's countless servitors
Nor can they ever be exempt
From his taxation of contempt.
So distantly I turn to view
The shamblings of that motley crew,
Those souls that hate the strength that mine has
Steeled in the school of old Aquinas.*
Where they have crouched and crawled and prayed
I stand the self-doomed, unafraid,
Unfellowed, friendless and alone,
Indifferent as the herring bone,
Firm as the mountain ridges where
I flash my antlers on the air.
Let them continue as is meet
To adequate the balance sheet.
Though they may labour to the grave
My spirit shall they never have

Nor make my soul with theirs at one
Till the Mahamanvantara* be done:
And though they spurn me from their door
My soul shall spurn them evermore.

(August 1904)

Gas from a Burner*

Ladies and gents, you are here assembled
To hear why earth and heaven trembled
Because of the black and sinister arts
Of an Irish writer in foreign parts.
He sent me a book ten years ago
I read it a hundred times or so,
Backwards and forwards, down and up,
Through both the ends of a telescope.
I printed it all to the very last word
But by the mercy of the Lord
The darkness of my mind was rent
And I saw the writer's foul intent.
But I owe a duty to Ireland:
I hold her honour in my hand,
This lovely land that always sent
Her writers and artists to banishment
And in a spirit of Irish fun
Betrayed her own leaders, one by one.
'Twas Irish humour, wet and dry,
Flung quicklime into Parnell's eye;*
'Tis Irish brains that save from doom
The leaky barge of the Bishop of Rome
For everyone knows the Pope can't belch
Without the consent of Billy Walsh.*
O Ireland my first and only love
Where Christ and Caesar are hand in glove!
O lovely land where the shamrock grows!
(Allow me, ladies, to blow my nose)

To show you for strictures I don't care a button
I printed the poems of Mountainy Mutton*
And a play* he wrote (you've read it, I'm sure)
Where they talk of "bastard", "bugger" and "whore".
And a play on the Word and Holy Paul
And some woman's legs that I can't recall
Written by Moore,* a genuine gent
That lives on his property's ten per cent:
I printed mystical books in dozens:
I printed the table book of Cousins*
Though (asking your pardon) as for the verse
'Twould give you a heartburn on your arse:
I printed folklore from North and South
By Gregory of the Golden Mouth:*
I printed poets, sad, silly and solemn:
I printed Patrick What-do-you-Colm:*
I printed the great John Milicent Synge*
Who soars above on an angel's wing
In the playboy shift* that he pinched as swag
From Maunsel's* manager's travelling bag.
But I draw the line at that bloody fellow,
That was over here dressed in Austrian yellow,
Spouting Italian* by the hour
To O'Leary Curtis* and John Wyse Power*
And writing of Dublin, dirty and dear,
In a manner no blackamoor printer could bear.
Shite and onions! Do you think I'll print
The name of the Wellington Monument,*
Sydney Parade and the Sandymount tram,
Downes's cakeshop and Williams's jam?
I'm damned if I do – I'm damned to blazes!
Talk about *Irish Names of Places*!*

It's a wonder to me, upon my soul,
He forgot to mention Curly's Hole.*
No, ladies, my press shall have no share in
So gross a libel on Stepmother Erin.*
I pity the poor – that's why I took
A red-headed Scotchman to keep my book.
Poor sister Scotland! Her doom is fell;
She cannot find any more Stuarts to sell.
My conscience is fine as Chinese silk:
My heart is as soft as buttermilk.
Colm* can tell you I made a rebate
Of one hundred pounds on the estimate
I gave him for his Irish Review.
I love my country – by herrings I do!
I wish you could see what tears I weep
When I think of the emigrant train and ship.
That's why I publish far and wide
My quite illegible railway guide.
In the porch of my printing institute
The poor and deserving prostitute
Plays every night at catch-as-catch-can
With her tight-breeched British artilleryman
And the foreigner learns the gift of the gab
From the drunken draggle-tail Dublin drab.
Who was it said: Resist not evil?*
I'll burn that book, so help me devil.
I'll sing a psalm as I watch it burn
And the ashes I'll keep in a one-handled urn.
I'll penance do with farts and groans
Kneeling upon my marrowbones.
This very next lent I will unbare
My penitent buttocks to the air

And sobbing beside my printing press
My awful sin I will confess.
My Irish foreman from Bannockburn*
Shall dip his right hand in the urn
And sign criss-cross with reverent thumb
*Memento homo** upon my bum.

Flushing, September 1912

Ecce Puer*

Of the dark past
A child is born;
With joy and grief
My heart is torn.

Calm in his cradle
The living lies.
May love and mercy
Unclose his eyes!

Young life is breathed
On the glass;
The world that was not
Comes to pass.

A child is sleeping:
An old man gone.
Oh, father forsaken,
Forgive your son!

(February 1932)

Note on the Text

Chamber Music and *Pomes Penyeach* were first published during James Joyce's lifetime. Six poems from *Chamber Music* (composed 1901–4) appeared individually in books or periodicals before the complete collection was published by Elkin Mathews in 1907. The composition of *Pomes Penyeach* dates from 1903–24, and the collection appeared in 1927 (Shakespeare and Company), before a corrected version was produced by Faber in 1933. Of the uncollected poems included in this volume, 'The Holy Office' (1904–5), 'Gas from a Burner' (1912) and 'Ecce Puer' (1932) were circulated during Joyce's lifetime. The rest of the poems in this volume first appeared in print within twenty-five years of his death in 1941, the majority in biographies or manuscript catalogues.

Spelling has been updated and standardized across the poems in this edition. Joyce's alterations of the text for the second and third editions of *Chamber Music* (published in 1918 and 1923 respectively) included the removal of hyphens for words such as "song-confessed". This volume follows the more standardized punctuation of the earlier version.

Notes

CHAMBER MUSIC

p. 1, CHAMBER MUSIC: The ambivalent title is supposedly a pun on the sound of urine tinkling in a chamber pot, reflecting Joyce's comments to his brother Stanislaus (1884–1955) in 1907 that he did not like the poems, but felt some of them were "pretty enough to be put to music". The collection consists largely of youthful love poems; Joyce gave a handwritten copy to his future wife Nora in 1909.

p. 27, *Oread*: The Oreads were mountain nymphs in Greek mythology.

p. 28, *In Purchas or in Holinshed*: Samuel Purchas (1577–1626), author of *Pilgrimes* (1624–25), a theological and geographical history of Asia, Africa and America; Raphael Holinshed (1529–1580?), author of *Chronicles of England, Scotland, and Ireland* (1577).

p. 29, *Mithridates*: Mithridates VI of Pontus (r.120–63 BC) built up an immunity to poison by administering it to himself in small doses.

p. 33, *Donneycarney*: A village outside Dublin where lovers often went to walk.

POMES PENYEACH

p. 39, POMES PENYEACH: The title plays on the French "*pomme*" ("apple"). The first edition was priced at twelve pence (one shilling) – the poems cost "a penny each". There are actually thirteen poems in the collection, but this is accounted for by the title of the first: "Tilly" (Irish "*tuilleadh*") means an "extra serving", so the poems come to an English "baker's dozen".

p. 41, *Cabra*: A suburb on the northern outskirts of Dublin, where the Joyce family lived from 1902–5.

p. 42, *San Sabba*: Near Trieste, where Joyce was largely based between 1904 and 1915.

p. 42, *No more, return no more*: A translation of the last line of Johnson's aria from Puccini's *La fanciulla del West*.

p. 44, *Rahoon*: A cemetery in Galway, where Nora's early admirer Michael Bodkin (1879–1900) was buried.

p. 45, *Tutto è sciolto*: "All is undone" (Italian). The words, pronounced by Elvino – who believes his bride-to-be Amina is faithless, having been caught sleepwalking in Rodolfo's room – are from Act Two of Vincenzo Bellini's (1801–35) *La sonnambula* (1831).

p. 46, *Fontana*: The Fountain of the Four Continents is located in Trieste's Piazza Unità d'Italia, which opens onto the harbour.

p. 47, *O bella bionda, / sei come l'onda*: The epigraph, which translates, "Beautiful blonde, / you are like a wave!" is adapted from a Trentine folk song: "*Come porti i capelli bella bionda! / Tu li porti alla bella marinara! / Tu li porti come l'onda, / come l'onda in mezzo al mar! // In mezzo al mar / ci stan camin che fumano; / saran della mia bella / che si consumano!*" ("I like the way you wear your locks! / You wear them like a beautiful mariner! / You wear them like a wave, / Like a wave of the sea! // In the middle of the sea / There are ships' funnels billowing; / They must belong to my darling, / and must be wearing thin!")

p. 52, *Bahnhofstrasse*: A street in Zurich where Joyce suffered his first attack of glaucoma.

p. 57, *George O'Donnell*: A school friend of Joyce's. Joyce wrote this poem on the front page of one of O'Donnell's schoolbooks.

p. 57, *Goldsmith*: Oliver Goldsmith (1728?–74), author of 'Retaliation' (1774), an unfinished poem containing a series of humorous epitaphs written for his close friends.

p. 57, *"murphies", spirits and 'baccy*: Potatoes, alcohol and tobacco.

p. 57, *Kilmainham*: A prison in County Dublin where many nationalist activists were held.

p. 57, *Drumcondra's production*: Drumcondra was the inner Dublin suburb where O'Donnell lived, and which the Joyce family had left as their financial situation worsened.

p. 57, *Portland jail*: A prison on the Isle of Portland, Dorset.

p. 58, *O fons Bandusiæ*: Joyce was able to quote Horace (65–8 BC) from memory after studying him in school. The Spring of Bandusia is supposed to have been located near Horace's hometown

Venusia (now Venosa), in the southern Italian region of Basilicata.

p. 59, *Chanson d'automne*: 'Autumn Song'. Paul Verlaine (1844–96) wrote it for the 'Paysages tristes' section of his first collection of poetry, *Poèmes saturniens* (1866).

p. 60, *Rudolf Goldschmidt*: An Austrian friend of Joyce's in Switzerland, who agreed to lend Claude Sykes (see note to p. 78) a typewriter from his office to use for the opening chapters of *Ulysses*.

p. 60, *Amorous Goldfish*: From the popular Edwardian musical comedy *The Geisha* (1896), whose score was composed by Sidney Jones (1861–1946) to a libretto by Owen Hall (1853–1907), with lyrics by Harry Greenbank (1865–99) and additional songs by other authors.

p. 60, *Kriegsverein*: Here used in semantic contrast with the *Hilfsverein* ("Benevolent Association") where Goldschmidt worked; so, as has been suggested by some critics, a translation such as "Malevolent Society" seems more suitable than a literal rendering ("war syndicate").

p. 60, *Schlachtfeld*: "Battlefield".

p. 60, *Donnerwet – wet – wetter*: *Donnerwetter* is a German word meaning "Chaos" (as, for example, in the expression "*Es wird ein schönes Donnerwetter geben*" – "All hell will break loose").

p. 61, *Miss Moschos*: Sister of a shop assistant acquainted with Joyce at Shakespeare and Company.

p. 62, *Dalton's Dilemma*: Referring to colour-blindness, early research into which was carried out by the scientist John Dalton (1766–1844), who was himself affected by the condition.

p. 62, *groening*: Middle Dutch *groen* is the etymological root of "green" (compare "roth", obsolete spelling of of Middle Low German *rot* = "red").

p. 62, *roth*: Samuel Roth (1893–1974) began publishing sections of Ulysses without permission in his magazine *Two Worlds*. "Roth" is also slang for "penis".

p. 62, *gage*: A reference to Crosby Gaige, who published the authorized edition of an early version of Joyce's *Finnegans Wake*, *Anna Livia Plurabelle*, in 1928 (see Extra Material, Joyce's Works, p. 107).

p. 63, *St James*: The poem is a rewriting of the nursery rhyme 'As I was going to St Ives'.

p. 64, *Pour la rîme seulement*: Translation: "To Pierre de Lanux. Said Valéry Larbaud, / Lend me a dux / Who can lead the assault. / My footsoldiers have melted / And are dying of faintness. / Be your *petit tondu* / For the glory of Ares. // Lanux de la Pierre / To Beaulard replied, / To hell with war / With your mercenaries. / So for Italy / Pack your bags, pronto, / Make the best of it / With some bullets. // At these words, Leryval / Rushes off in his armoured coach / And, like old Hannibal, / Smashes through the blockade, / Shows hardly any distress / When one shouts to high heaven, / One under Mursoline / For the arrest of glory."

p. 64, *pioupions*: An alternative translation could be "squaddies" or "grunts", preserving the original low register.

p. 64, *fondus*: Literally "melted", but could also be translated as "cast".

p. 64, *malaise*: Could also be translated as "discomfort" or "disease".

p. 64, *petit tondu*: Napoleon Bonaparte's nickname (cf. "dux", alluding to Mussolini).

p. 64, *soldiqués*: More colloquial and pejorative than "mercenaries".

p. 64, *obobus*: Could also be translated as "missile coach".

p. 64, *Mursoline*: Mussolini (cf. "dux").

p. 64, *arrats*: Phonetically close to "arrêt" ("stop").

p. 65, *Ghosts*: An 1881 play by Norwegian playwright Henrik Ibsen (1828–1906). The play addresses taboo subjects such as incest and venereal disease, as the syphilitic Oswald, whose illness was passed down from his father, falls in love with his illegitimate half-sister Regina. Their family relationship comes to light as the sexual misdemeanours of their father, the late Captain Alving, are exposed.

p. 65, *grim old grouser*: Ibsen.

p. 65, *the lewd knight*: Falstaff, a character from Shakespeare's *The Merry Wives of Windsor*.

p. 65, *His quantum sat of Pox Romana*: "His fill of the Pox" (playing on *Pax Romana*, the treaty which held the Roman Empire together).

p. 66, *YMCA, VD, TB*: Young Men's Christian Association, Venereal Disease, Tuberculosis.

p. 67, *Lebendig begraben*: A collection of fourteen poems by Swiss poet and novelist Gottfried Keller (1819–90). Joyce heard Othmar Schoeck's (1886–1957) musical settings of the poems on a visit to Zurich.

p. 68, *Madame Jolas*: The Jolases had invited Joyce to dinner on Thanksgiving Day (25th November 1937) in Neuilly, west of Paris. He heard that the turkey had been dropped on the way back from the market, and that its liver had been lost.

p. 68, *Grand Palais Potin*: Félix Potin (1820–71) gave his name to a Parisian retail chain he founded in the mid-nineteenth century.

p. 68, *Lieber's code*: German-American jurist Franz Lieber (1789–1872) wrote the *Lieber Code* in 1863, a comprehensive code of conduct for soldiers in the field, including regulations protecting civilians and prisoners.

p. 68, *swanee way*: Referring to Stephen Foster's song 'Swanee River', written from the perspective of a slave wanting to go "home" to the plantation where he worked all his life.

p. 68, *Octroi*: Toll booth at the entrance to a city.

p. 68, *Holy Poule*: *Poule* is French slang for "young woman", literally "hen". "Holy Poule" is homophonic with the Dublin expression "Holy Paul".

p. 68, *Loye*: *L'oie* = "goose".

p. 69, *Osmanli*: Ottomans.

p. 69, *hommes*: Men.

p. 69, *mujik*: A Russian peasant, here referring to the Jolases' servant Conrad.

p. 69, *Madamina*: "Madame" combined with "Balamina" (a favourite song of Marie Jolas's).

p. 69, *Big Noise*: Franklin D. Roosevelt (1882–1945), President of the USA from 1933 until his death.

p. 69, *That Turco's talking straight*: A reference to the pantomime *Turco the Terrible*, which was first performed in Dublin in 1873.

p. 70, *John Quinn*: New York lawyer and collector John Quinn (1870–1924) bought the manuscript of Joyce's play *Exiles* in 1917, which Joyce sent in two instalments. He later bought the manuscript of *Ulysses*, and acted as its legal defender after the US Post Office declared it "obscene", though Joyce felt his defence was inadequate.

p. 71, *Claude Sykes*: A Zurich-based actor (1883–1964) who typed *Ulysses*, and a mountaineering enthusiast. Joyce did not share this interest, but both liked comic verse. Joyce sent the first four limericks in this section to Sykes.

p. 72, *Simeone Levi*: A pupil of Joyce's in Zurich. The title refers to the popular song 'Solomon Levi' (1885), words and music by Fred Seaver.

p. 73, *D.L.G.*: David Lloyd George (1863–1945) was UK Prime Minister 1916–22.

p. 73, *Bully*: John Bull, personification of the UK.

p. 74, *P.J.T.*: Irish painter Patrick (Joseph) Tuohy (1894–1930) painted Joyce's brother Stanislaus in Dublin in 1923, and Joyce himself in Paris the following year.

p. 75, *Holy Office*: The Christian office of confession. The "Supreme Sacred Congregation of the Holy Office" was the name given to the institution of the Catholic Inquisition, established in the Middle Ages to suppress heresy. The poem takes aim at Joyce's contemporaries on the Irish literary scene, denouncing them as hypocritical romantics.

p. 75, *Katharsis-Purgative*: Katharsis is Greek for "cleansing".

p. 75, *Aristotle*: Joyce posits himself on the side of Aristotle in conflict with his Platonic contemporaries.

p. 75, *Peripatetic*: Aristotelian school of philosophy.

p. 75, *Dante*: Joyce respected Dante as a writer committed to a cause, working in defiance of the authorities. He scorned reductive secular interpretations of Dante by modern critics, who considered themselves "Dante without the unfortunate prejudices of Dante".

p. 75, *mumming company*: Alluding to the Abbey Theatre, at the centre of the Irish literary and cultural circle at the time.

p. 75, *With him... appease*: The Irish poet W.B. Yeats (1865–1939).

p. 75, *giddy dames*: Referring to Annie Horniman (1860–1937), theatre patron who established the Abbey Theatre, and Lady Gregory (1852–1932), its manager, among others.

p. 75, *gold-embroidered Celtic fringes*: Referring to the elaborate decoration of Yeats's 1890s publications.

p. 76, *Or him... day*: Abbey playwright John Millington Synge (1871–1909).

p. 76, *naggin*: Irish word for a bottle of spirits. Drinking appears as a recognizable feature of Synge's work.

p. 76, *Or him... "tone"*: Irish poet and author Oliver St John Gogarty (1878–1957).

p. 76, *Or him... past*: Irish poet, novelist and playwright Padraic Colum (1881–1972), who in 1903 was granted a three-year patronage by an American millionaire to write about rural life.

p. 76, *Or him... courtesy*: The Irish author and librarian W.K. Magee (1868–1961).

p. 76, *Or him... dear*: The Irish poet and Abbey actor George Roberts (1873–1953), follower of the writer George Russell (pseudonym Æ, 1867–1935).

p. 76, *Or him... fear*: The Irish poet Seamus O'Sullivan (1879–1958).

p. 76, *Or him... Aeschylus*: Russell (see the note before the one above).

p. 76, *My scarlet*: "Though your sins be as scarlet, they shall be as white as snow" (Isaiah 1:18).

p. 76, *vicar-general*: A priest who represents the Bishop in local affairs within his diocese.

p. 77, *Mammon*: New Testament personification of material wealth.

p. 77, *Leviathan*: Quasi-Satanic sea monster referred to in the Old Testament.

p. 77, *Aquinas*: St Thomas Aquinas (1225–74), who embraced Aristotelian philosophy in conjunction with Christian teachings, and whose integrity Joyce admired.

p. 78, *Mahamanvantara*: "Great year" in Sanskrit, referring to a life cycle or period of evolution of the universe.

p. 79, *Gas from a Burner*: Joyce signed a contract with Maunsel and Company in 1909 for the publication of *Dubliners*. The manager, George Roberts (see sixth note to p. 76), held up the publication for three years, demanding that Joyce amend his use of real names for people and places. Joyce eventually offered to purchase the unpublished sheets of the first edition, but the printer, John Falconer, destroyed them when he heard of the dispute (see Extra Material, Joyce's Life, p. 92). Joyce wrote 'Gas from a Burner' in response; the speaker is largely a combination of Roberts and Falconer.

p. 79, *Parnell's eye*: A reference to Charles Stewart Parnell (1846–91), a towering figure in the Irish Home Rule movement. The Home Rule Party split in 1891, as anti-Parnellites revolted against his leadership. See Extra Material, Joyce's Life, p. 89.

p. 79, *Billy Walsh*: William J. Walsh (1841–1921), Roman Catholic Archbishop of Dublin 1885–1921 and nationalist sympathizer.

p. 80, *Mountainy Mutton*: Maunsel and Company published *The Mountainy Singer* by Joseph Campbell (1881–1944) in 1909.

p. 80, *a play*: Maunsel published Campbell's *Judgment*, uncensored, in 1912.

p. 80, *Moore*: The Anglo-Irish writer George Moore (1852–1933), author of *The Apostle* (1911), which describes fictional conversations between Christ and Paul, and explores sensual language in the Bible. The "woman's legs" are Bathsheba's, which caught King David's attention.

p. 80, *table book of Cousins*: The Irish writer James H. Cousins (1873–1956), whose *Etain the Beloved and Other Poems* Maunsel and Company published in 1912.

p. 80, *Gregory of the Golden Mouth*: Maunsel and Company published books by Lady Gregory in 1909; "golden mouth" recalls her dental fillings and ironically links her to St John "Chrysostom" (309–407 AD), whose epithet "golden-mouthed" refers to his eloquence.

p. 80, *Patrick What-do-you-Colm*: Padraic Colum (see fourth note to p. 76).

p. 80, *John Milicent Synge*: John Millington Synge (see first note to p. 76).

p. 80, *playboy shift*: Synge's play *Playboy of the Western World* scandalized the Abbey Theatre in 1907. Among the lines considered most offensive was "a drift of chosen females, standing in their shifts".

p. 80, *Maunsel's*: Maunsel and Company's (see title note).

p. 80, *dressed in Austrian yellow, / Spouting Italian*: Joyce lived in Trieste, where Italian was spoken, but which was occupied by Austria at the time of his writing.

p. 80, *O'Leary Curtis*: A reference to a Dublin journalist.

p. 80, *John Wyse Power*: Journalist and Irish nationalist (1859–1926).

p. 80, *Wellington Monument... cakeshop*: Dublin toponyms explicitly mentioned in *Dubliners*.

p. 80, *Irish Names of Places*: P.W. Joyce, *The Origin and History of Irish Names of Places* (1869), a standard school book at the time (and in which 'Satire on George O'Donnell' was written).

p. 81, *Curly's Hole*: A bathing pool in the Dublin suburb of Dollymount.

p. 81, *Stepmother Erin*: from "Éirinn", the dative of the Irish word for Ireland. Roberts was an Ulster Scot, making Ireland his "stepmother".

p. 81, *Colm*: Padraic Colum (see fourth note to p. 76).

p. 81, *Resist not evil*: Christ's words during the Sermon on the Mount (Matthew 5:39).

p. 82, *Bannockburn*: A town in Scotland where Robert the Bruce (1274–1329) defeated the English in 1314.

p. 82, *Memento homo*: "*Memento, homo, quia pulvis es*" ("Remember, man, that thou art dust"), spoken by priests on Ash Wednesday while marking a sign of the cross in ashes on each penitent's forehead.

p. 83, *Ecce Puer*: "Behold the Boy". The poem was written on 15th February 1932, the day Joyce's grandson was born after a difficult pregnancy for Joyce's daughter Helen, and nine days after the death of Joyce's father.

Extra Material

on

James Joyce's

Chamber Music

and Other Poems

James Joyce's Life

James Joyce was born on 2nd February 1882 in *Birth and Political*
Rathgar, a suburb of Dublin, and was the eldest *Background*
surviving child of what became a large family. His
childhood saw the decline of both Ireland's for-
tunes and his family's. The Act of Union, imposed
in 1800, had wrested economic and political control
away from Ireland towards England, leaving behind
an impoverished and destitute land. The dominant
socio-political event of Joyce's childhood was the
political demise of Charles Stewart Parnell, the fore-
most figure of the Irish Home Rule movement. Parnell
had been successful in advancing the cause of Irish
independence from British rule until 1889, when he
was accused of having an adulterous affair with the
wife of one of his political associates. The ensuing
scandal diminished him politically, and he died in
1891. Joyce's father, John Stanislaus, was an ardent
Parnellite and benefited from his party's patronage.
On the occasion of Parnell's death, Joyce, then just
nine years old, wrote a poem entitled 'Et tu, Healy',
which condemned Parnell's foes from within his own
party. John Stanislaus was so proud of his son for this
that he had copies privately printed, although none
of these broadsides are known to survive. John Joyce
blamed his own declining fortunes on anti-Parnellite
forces, although his propensity to drink was the more
likely cause. At the time of his first son's birth, in
addition to having inherited significant property in
Cork, John Joyce was a prosperous collector of rates,

but by the 1890s his wealth was so diminished that he often moved his family to new houses surreptitiously to avoid rapacious debt collectors. His son would inherit this peripatetic lifestyle.

Education   Joyce was educated first at the Clongowes Wood Jesuit school in County Kildare from the age of six and a half to nine, when he had to leave, because his father could no longer afford the fees. John Stanislaus was then able to secure a place for his son at another Jesuit school, free of charge: Belvedere College in Dublin. Joyce's university years were at the Royal University (now University College Dublin), yet another Jesuit institution. At college he was regarded as one of the most brilliant students of his generation, and Joyce later credited the Jesuits for imparting to him his critical and intellectual skills.

Move to Paris   Upon his graduation from college, Joyce moved to Paris, ostensibly with the aim of studying medicine, but with the secret ambition of becoming a writer. By early 1904 he had written a brief philosophical and autobiographical sketch entitled 'A Portrait of the Artist', which, like many of his subsequent works, was rejected for publication.

Return to Dublin   In April 1903, while he was still in Paris, his mother became seriously ill and he was called back to Dublin. She died on 13th August 1903. The following June, while walking on Nassau Street, by Trinity College, he met a young woman from Galway named Nora Barnacle, who was working as a maid in a nearby hotel. Their first date was on 16th June. Joyce commemorated this event by setting *Ulysses* on this day.

While she became his lifelong companion, they did not marry until 1931.

Dismayed by the political and cultural environment in *Move to Trieste* Ireland, Joyce planned to exile himself to the Continent. Having persuaded Nora to join him, they left Dublin in October 1904 and eventually settled in Trieste, where he took a position teaching English at the Berlitz School. Apart from a few months in Rome in 1906 and 1907, Joyce and Nora stayed in Trieste until shortly after the outbreak of the First World War. Joyce eventually persuaded his younger brother Stanislaus, with whom he had a difficult relationship, and two of his sisters to join them in Trieste. A son, Giorgio, was born in 1905 and a daughter, Lucia, in 1907.

In Trieste, Joyce continued to write poems *Early Writing* (eventually collected into the volume *Chamber Music*) as well as short stories for his collection *Dubliners*. While in Rome he planned to add a story to *Dubliners* called 'Ulysses', but he admitted that work on that story never progressed beyond its title. Before he left Dublin, he had begun work on expanding his essay 'A Portrait of the Artist' into a novel called *Stephen Hero*, a fictionalized autobiography of his youth in Dublin. By the summer of 1905 he had abandoned *Stephen Hero* only to restart it as *A Portrait of the Artist as a Young Man* in 1907. The earlier novel was written in a more or less straightforward narrative style, whereas the second version has a much more innovative structure and clearly exhibits the influence of continental European writers such as Flaubert and D'Annunzio.

Dubliners   Joyce had great difficulty in getting *Dubliners* published. After considerable back-and-forth between publishers in London and Dublin, Joyce returned to Dublin in 1912 to meet with George Roberts of the firm Maunsel and Company to try to persuade him to publish his book. Joyce was not just unsuccessful in persuading him: Roberts's printer, offended by Joyce's book, actually destroyed the page proofs. Joyce was so outraged at this that he never again returned to Dublin. Fortunately, the following year, Grant Richards, a publisher in London, offered to publish *Dubliners* despite having rejected it previously.

A Portrait of the Artist   In July 1915 Joyce and Nora fled war-torn Trieste for
as a Young Man and   neutral Zurich, where he continued work on *Ulysses*,
Publication Difficulties   the novel he began after completing *A Portrait*. The
with Ulysses   latter was finally published, after some difficulty, in the US in 1916 and in the UK in 1917. (Joyce wrote a play, *Exiles*, in 1914, in between *A Portrait* and *Ulysses*.) *Ulysses* was published in serialization in two journals in 1918, *The Egoist* in the UK and *The Little Review* in the US. Because of fear of being prosecuted for publishing material deemed obscene, *The Egoist* only published four episodes of *Ulysses*. *The Little Review* was able to publish the first thirteen episodes and a portion of the fourteenth, before they were prosecuted by the New York Society for the Prevention of Vice in 1920. This trial scared off prospective publishers on both sides of the Atlantic. By this time Joyce and his family had moved to Paris, and he found himself with no feasible prospect of having *Ulysses* published in an English-speaking country unless he would consent to

removing the more contentious portions. Adamantly opposed to this, he was able to arrange to have *Ulysses* published in Paris through the bookshop Shakespeare and Company, which was run by Sylvia Beach, an expatriate American.

Joyce had a patron, something which is most *Financial* unusual for a modern author. Starting in 1917, *Assistance* Harriet Shaw Weaver, the principal editor for *The Egoist*, would send Joyce instalments of money. At first these were anonymous; she revealed herself as his benefactor in 1919. Weaver's contributions to Joyce helped him through the difficult years when he was a writer struggling to get his work published and continued for the rest of his life. Without her assistance, Joyce would not have been able to get *Ulysses* published.

Ulysses was published in France on 2nd February *Publication of* 1922, Joyce's fortieth birthday. The date was decided *Ulysses* upon when Maurice Darantière, the printer, informed Joyce and Beach that Joyce's continual revisions meant that the original publication date of November 1921 was impossible.

In early 1932, Bennett Cerf of Random House secured the American rights to *Ulysses* and, sensing that the moral landscape of the United States had changed, began planning its publication. The following autumn, *Ulysses* was again put on trial, but this time with a favourable outcome, and *Ulysses* was finally published in the United States in 1934, more than a decade after the Paris printing. A British edition, published by the Bodley Head, followed in 1936.

Finnegans Wake and Death   The publication of *Ulysses* and its ensuing controversy ensured Joyce's reputation as one of the major writers of the twentieth century. He began his next book in 1922. This was published in serial form in a variety of journals (but, after 1927, primarily in the journal *transition*) under the title *Work in Progress*. Its final title, *Finnegans Wake*, was kept secret from all except Nora until its publication in 1939. With the onset of the Second World War the Joyces fled Paris, first for Saint-Gérand-le-Puy, a small village in unoccupied France, and then for Zurich, where Joyce died on 13th January 1941, after complications following surgery. Although the Irish government did not send a representative to his funeral, Joyce's passing did not go unmarked in his home country. In their obituary notice, the *Irish Times* called Joyce "an Irishman of the Irish [...] the complete Dubliner".

– Sam Slote

James Joyce's Works

Dubliners   Finally appearing in volume form in 1914, *Dubliners* had a complicated publication history. Three of the stories – 'The Sisters', 'Eveline' and 'After the Race' – were completed as early as 1904 and published separately in the *Irish Homestead* journal that same year. In 1905, the tales, along with nine others, were accepted for publication as a collection by Grant Richards in London. However, when the book was typeset, Richards's printer refused to print 'Two

Gallants' and wanted certain passages in other stories to be modified, in order to avoid prosecution under England's obscenity laws. The publication was cancelled, and Joyce submitted the collection (augmented from twelve to fifteen tales) to various houses until it was finally accepted in 1909 by Maunsel and Company of Dublin. However, the project was again abandoned after the firm objected to the political nature of some of the content. After a number of further unsuccessful submissions, Joyce managed to secure another deal with Grant Richards, who published *Dubliners* in 1914, using a copy of the proofs Joyce had salvaged from Maunsel as the copy text.

Although there are some recurring characters in the fifteen short stories of the *Dubliners*, the pieces are largely independent but unified by the setting – Joyce's contemporary Dublin – and by the fact that they all more or less feature an epiphanic experience. In the overall structure there is also an evolution from youth to maturity, as the protagonists and narrators of the story get progressively older.

In 'The Sisters', a boy comes down to supper and learns from Old Cotter, a friend of the family, that Father Flynn, who had been his mentor, has died of a stroke. The conversation moves on to discuss the negative influence the priest has had on the boy, which baffles the latter, who that night dreams of the deceased. The next day the boy passes by Father Flynn's house, sees a notice announcing his death and feels a sense of liberation. That evening he goes to view the corpse at the house of mourning and hears his aunt talking to Father Flynn's sisters about their brother, hinting at his odd behaviour and a scandal he was potentially involved in.

'An Encounter' deals with two boys – the narrator and his friend Mahony – who decide to skip school on a warm summer day and happen to meet an old man who asks them about their education and love lives, before moving away to masturbate. Mahony leaves to follow a stray cat, while the stranger returns and launches into a rant to the narrator about misbehaving and needing to be punished. When the old man leaves again, the narrator goes to find his friend.

In 'Araby', a young boy becomes infatuated with the sister of his neighbour Mangan, and promises to buy her something from a temporary bazaar which gives its name to the story. Unfortunately, on the day of the event, the boy's uncle comes home late, which means that he does not make it to the bazaar on time and does not manage to purchase anything.

The eponymous protagonist of 'Eveline' is a young woman reminiscing about her childhood and hesitating about her decision to elope to Argentina with a sailor called Frank, as this would mean leaving her family, including her drunkard father, with whom she has a difficult relationship. When she arrives at the docks later that day, she decides to stay in Ireland and leaves Frank to board the ferry alone.

In 'After the Race', after watching an automobile race on the outskirts of Dublin, the young man Jimmy Doyle joins the drivers of the French team and an Englishman called Routh on the yacht of Farley, a rich American. On board they celebrate and play cards, at which Jimmy loses a considerable amount of money.

'Two Gallants' tells the tale of Corley and Lenehan, who plan to take advantage of a housemaid who works in a wealthy household. While Corley leaves with her, Lenehan ambles through Dublin and stops to have dinner, before observing the woman enter a house through the basement and come out through the front door. Corley then shows him a gold coin she has purloined from the house.

In 'The Boarding House', the proprietor of the eponymous establishment, Mrs Mooney, observes as her daughter Polly is being courted by one of the lodgers, the clerk Mr Doran. When some of the other guests start noticing the romance, Mrs Mooney confronts him and insists that he must marry Polly. As he feels guilty and fears the reactions of his employer and Polly's brother Jack, Mr Doran agrees to take her as his wife, despite not loving her and her being of a lower social status.

'A Little Cloud' opens with the clerk and aspiring poet Little Chandler going to meet his friend Gallaher – who is in Dublin having left eight years previously to pursue a successful career as a journalist in London – at a restaurant for dinner. After having listened to Gallaher's account of his life and fantasizing about achieving similar success himself, Little Chandler returns to his wife and baby and ends up feeling shame about his escapist thoughts and reconciling himself to his situation.

In 'Counterparts', the clerk Farrington is put to shame by his boss, and decides to pawn his watch in order to spend the evening drinking in pubs. He returns home from the night of revelry in an even fouler temper, and vents his frustration by beating one of his children.

'Clay' tells the story of Maria, an employee in the kitchen of a charitable institution, who goes to attend a Hallowe'en party hosted by Joe Donnelly, whom she used to nurse when he was a child. When she arrives, she realizes with some frustration that she has forgotten the plum cake she had bought for the occasion. She plays traditional Hallowe'en games – one of which involves her choosing a piece of clay while blindfolded, a harbinger of imminent death – and sings a song for the company.

In 'A Painful Case', the solitary bank clerk James Duffy meets the married Mrs Sinico at a concert, and the two grow chastely attached to each other. At one of their meetings she reaches out for his hand and he decides to break off the relationship. When, four years later, he reads in a newspaper that she has died – possibly by committing suicide – he begins to feel guilty and finds himself imagining her life of sadness and loneliness.

'Ivy Day in the Committee Room' takes place during a local election, when Mr O'Connor, a canvasser for one of the candidates, sits in the committee room and has conversations with fellow promoters. As it is Ivy Day, which commemorates the death of Charles Parnell, the discussions give way to a patriotic poem recited by Joe Hynes in honour of the deceased nationalist politician.

In 'A Mother', Mrs Kearney, who has arranged with Mr Holohan, the secretary of a cultural society, for her daughter to play in a series of four concerts, tries to extract payment from the latter, as things have not been going to plan, a process which holds up the final performance. After failing to receive sufficient assurances from Mr Holohan and other members of the society, she refuses to let her daughter play in the second half.

'Grace' deals with the businessman Tom Kernan, the day after he got drunk and lost consciousness, as he talks in his bedroom with his friends, who want to take him to a retreat where he can surmount his alcohol problems. After much discussion and gossip, they go to the retreat and listen to a sermon by a priest.

'The Dead' is the longest and most famous piece in *Dubliners*. Its main character is the professor Gabriel Conroy, who attends a party organized by his two elderly aunts, Julia and Kate Morkan, with his wife Gretta. At the event, he dances with a teacher, Miss Ivors, who provokes him, and delivers a short speech. At the end of the evening he witnesses Gretta listen in captivation to a song by the famous tenor Bartell D'Arcy, a sight which inflames his love and attraction for her. In the couple's hotel room later that night, Gretta confesses to Gabriel that she had been thinking of Michael Furey, a former lover who had died in his youth out of passion for her. This news is at once devastating for Gabriel, as he realizes that her feelings towards him will never live up to the ones inspired by Michael, and enlightening, as he sees in this situation a kind of revelation about life. The husband-and-wife relationship described in 'The Dead' would later inspire Joyce's only theatre play, *Exiles*, published in 1918. The story was also adapted into a film in 1987, *The Dead*, directed by John Huston.

Although *Dubliners* is Joyce's most accessible work and not as stylistically ambitious or experimental as his subsequent prose offerings (for example it features none of the mimetic and stream-of-consciousness techniques which made him a pioneer of Modernism), the stories, while deceptively simple, display an early mastery of description, dialogue and characterization, while also offering a vivid portrait of Ireland at the turn of the century. The collection has been compared by some to Picasso's early realist paintings, in which the artist honed his techniques according to traditional guidelines before embarking on formal experimentation.

A Portrait of the Artist as a Young Man   James Joyce's first novel, *A Portrait of the Artist as a Young Man*, was first published in instalments in *The Egoist* in 1914–15, before appearing in volume form first in the US (1916) and then the UK (1917). The basis for the semi-autobiographical *Künstlerroman* was the earlier story *Stephen Hero*, which Joyce had abandoned in 1905, before recasting it, in a much more experimental and ambitious version, as *A Portrait of the Artist as a Young Man*.

The novel covers the life of the young Dubliner Stephen Dedalus (based on Joyce himself) from roughly the age of three to the age of twenty, the emphasis being more on his intellectual and emotional development and the description of the narrator's epiphanic moments than on plot, strictly speaking. The narrative begins with Stephen's evocation of his childhood memories, which consists of fragments of perceptions and conversations, before moving on to describe his life at Clongowes Wood College, a Jesuit boarding school, where he is bullied by a classmate who pushes him into a stream, causing a prolonged stay in the school infirmary, where he begins to realize that he is an outsider. After the description of a Christmas dinner back home, during which Stephen is initially delighted to be sitting with the adults but subsequently dismayed by their bickering about politics, another formative school incident is recounted, in which Stephen is unjustly punished by the prefect of studies and successfully gets the rector to intervene in his favour, thereby gaining the approbation and admiration of his fellow pupils.

After a summer holiday he is told that he can no longer attend Clongowes Wood, due to his father's worsening finances (a revelation which mortifies the young Stephen), and is sent to Belvedere College, a Jesuit day school. There he distinguishes himself by his essay-writing and his acting in school productions, but he increasingly feels alienated from his peers and starts to doubt his Catholic faith. He also loses respect for his father, who has become an alcoholic and an irritating nostalgic, on a trip to Cork. Having attempted to use some prize money he had received for academic achievement to enhance his family's life, Stephen loses his virginity at the age of fourteen to a Dublin prostitute.

Racked by guilt at his perceived sin, he attends a Catholic retreat, during which he experiences terror at the sermons he hears describing the torments of hell. He is comforted by a sympathetic Capuchin monk and pledges to lead a life of purity. He briefly considers entering the clergy, but, after a moment of revelation when he sees a young woman bathing in the sea, he decides to focus on his artistic vocation. The rest of the novel deals at length with the thoughts and conversations from his time as a student, during which he notices how different he is from his peers, refuses to adhere strictly to either nationalist patriotism or Catholicism and elaborates his own aesthetic theories. At the end of the book he comes to the realization that in order to thrive artistically he must go abroad and sever his ties with Ireland.

With *A Portrait*, Joyce moved into the sphere of Modernism, of which he would become the figurehead. The novel makes abundant use of stream-of-consciousness narration and various techniques which mimic the narrator's perceptions, while also self-consciously adopting existing literary registers. It is also notably dense in its symbols and allusion to myth and other cultural references.

Ulysses *Ulysses* was first published in volume form in a French edition in 1922, after an obscenity trial had cut short its serialization in *The Little Review* in the US. The book remained banned for sale in the UK until the 1930s. Due to various attempts at correcting printing errors, the book has undergone several revisions during and after the author's lifetime, with the 1984 Gabler edition coming closest to being an authoritative edition, despite it having a number of detractors.

Ulysses, although a quarter of a million words in length and featuring a plethora of characters, styles and viewpoints, describes the events of just one single day, 16th June 1904, in Dublin, focusing mainly on the characters of Stephen Dedalus (the protagonist of *A Portrait* after he has come back from living abroad) and, for the bulk of the novel, the older Leopold Bloom, a half-Jewish advertising canvasser.

The book begins at around eight in the morning, with Stephen (the protagonist of the first three chapters out of eighteen) getting ready for the day with his housemates, the students Mulligan and Haines, before he goes to teach at a school, reflecting during a recitation about his own literary aspirations, followed by a contemplative walk on the seafront.

Leopold Bloom then becomes the focus of the narration, and the time shifts back to 8 a.m., as he goes to the butcher's and returns home to make breakfast for himself and his wife Molly (an aspiring singer who is having an affair with her manager Blazes Boylan), before setting off through Dublin to attend the funeral of Paddy Dignam, running errands, having conversations and reflecting on life, death and his personal history on the way.

After the funeral, Bloom enters the offices of the *Freeman's Journal* to try to place an advertisement with the paper, which proves unsuccessful. Coincidentally, Stephen Dedalus also goes there to deliver a letter from the head of his school. Bloom then continues his wandering, stopping to have lunch at a pub and meeting more acquaintances, such as Mrs Breen, who informs him that a mutual friend, Mrs Purefoy, is in the maternity hospital.

The next chapter (9) sees Stephen at the National Library in conversation about Shakespeare and literary theory with the library's director and other literati, while the one after that takes the shape of nineteen short vignettes focusing on a variety of protagonists, such as Stephen's sisters, Blazes Boylan, the Lord Lieutenant William Humble heading a procession and a miscellany of unrelated characters.

By the next chapter (11), Bloom is back in the frame, having an afternoon meal in the concert room of the Ormond Hotel, with Stephen's uncle, while listening to Simon Dedalus, Stephen's father, singing and thinking of Molly and Blazes Boylan, who he knows are having an encounter at the same time. He then goes to Barney Kiernan's pub where, in a chapter related by an unknown narrator, he has an argument with the staunch nationalist and anti-Semite character called the Citizen.

The scene then shifts to the beach at 8 p.m., where Gerty MacDowell is sitting next to her friends Edy Boardman and Cissy Caffrey – as well as the latter's younger brothers who are playing with a ball – while daydreaming romantically. When a fireworks display begins, she then exposes her underwear to the nearby Bloom, who masturbates. Then at 10 p.m. the latter visits Mina Purefoy in the maternity hospital, before following the drunk Stephen and his friends into Bella Cohen's brothel.

The brothel scene constitutes the longest chapter of the novel, and many hallucinations, thoughts and flashbacks are described at length. At the end, Stephen runs out and gets into trouble with British soldiers, with Bloom and the undertaker defusing the situation. In the next chapter Bloom and Stephen have coffee at a cabman's shelter and have conversations with locals before they go back in the penultimate chapter to Bloom's house, where Stephen declines an invitation to stay and leaves.

The final chapter deals with Molly's stream-of-consciousness thoughts as she is drifting to sleep, reflecting on her career, her husband and her lover. The novel ends on a hopeful, positive note.

One of the most ambitious books of world literature and the pinnacle of Modernism, *Ulysses* developed and went beyond the innovations offered by *A Portrait of the Artist as a Young Man*. It gives even more free rein to stream-of-consciousness, while at the same time providing a bafflingly comprehensive compendium of modes of speech and writing – ranging from the colloquial to the journalistic, scientific and musical, while encompassing a vast array of literary styles. The proliferation of allusions, symbols and wordplay has fuelled extensive critical apparatuses which rival the size of the book itself, not to mention countless academic discussions and treatises.

Finnegans Wake, Joyce's last novel, was the *Finnegans Wake* result of a seventeen-year process, and was first published in volume form in 1939. Instalments had been appearing as *Work in Progress* in *The*

Transatlantic Review and *transition* journals from 1924 onwards, although the title was not revealed until the book itself came out.

In terms of "plot" or "character", *Finnegans Wake* is even more difficult to describe than its predecessors. It is structured in four books, modelled on the conception of history as a cyclical succession of four ages – the age of gods, the age of heroes, the age of man and the *ricorso* or return to the beginning – expounded by the philosopher Giambattista Vico in his 1725 *Scienza nuova*. The first three parts are divided into subordinate four-chapter cycles that follow the same pattern and, furthermore, as the novel itself opens and ends in mid-sentence, it can in theory be read as a never-ending loop.

In substance, the book appears to be a lengthy description, eschewing any sense of chronology or fixed physical space, of a dream – although this statement and the following summary are just common interpretations of *Finnegans Wake* – the surreal logic of which is mimicked by the language used, with many invented, borrowed or portmanteau words and confusing stream-of-consciousness sentence structures. Although this is never made entirely clear, the dream ostensibly occurs on one night, in which Mr Porter (possibly the dreamer himself), his wife Ann, his daughter and his sons Kevin and Jerry are asleep in their house. This anchoring layer of reality sporadically seems to manifest itself by the recurring evocation of the sound of branches on the windows, and the parents briefly checking on the sons or apparently making love in the morning.

But mostly the dream/text transforms these characters into different ones, adding layers of mythology, universality and self-referentiality.

Mr Porter for example seemingly becomes Humphrey Chimpden Earwicker (or just "HCE"), the owner of a Dublin tavern who has been caught by soldiers in the act of peeping at two women and who is afflicted by an incestuous desire for his daughter. He in turn takes on the guises of Finnegan (the protagonist of a folk song), the mythical Irish warrior Finn MacCool, Adam, Noah, Moses, the Flying Dutchman, Parnell, among other more indeterminate incarnations, even non-human ones.

Mrs Porter also appears to morph into Anna Livia Plurabelle (ALP) and her presence also manifests itself as Eve, Isis, Mary and various rivers, phases of the moon and colours of the rainbow, while her sons become Shem and Shaun, two staunch rivals – the former embodying the artistic (for example as Penman – a parody of Joyce himself – or Lucifer) and the latter the political (as Postman, Jute or the Angel Michael). The conflicts between the two are described at length. And there are other characters, such as twelve customers of Earwicker's pub, four judges and three soldiers, who are reflected in numerous additional incarnations.

By far the most opaque and impenetrable of Joyce's prose works, *Finnegans Wake* takes the level of experimentation to such a height that only the most ambitious readers and most committed academics have been able to tackle it. Upon publication it received an overwhelming negative reception, and although it has since achieved the status of indisputable avant-garde masterpiece, its difficulty means that it is shunned by the general public, despite the efforts of its most eloquent supporters, such as Anthony Burgess, who claimed it reached unrivalled heights of comedy and beauty, and Harold Bloom, who ranked it on a level with the masterpieces of Dante and Shakespeare.

Poetry   In addition to his prose, Joyce also wrote and published poetry throughout his career. His first collection, *Chamber Music* (a title which he later facetiously claimed referred to the sound of urine tinkling on a chamber pot), appeared in 1907, containing thirty-six love poems. Although the book was by no means a commercial success, its verse was generally praised for its subtlety and emotional qualities. Twenty years later he published *Pomes Penyeach* (i.e. "poems penny each"), a volume containing thirteen poems – again mainly concerning love – which had been initially rejected for publication by Ezra Pound. Although this collection also did not attract much attention at the time, it contains some of his most famous verse creations, such as 'Tilly', 'A Flower Given to My Daughter' and 'Bahnhofstrasse'.

Publication Details for the Uncollected Poems

Satire on George O'Donnell
  Colum & Colum, *Our Friend James Joyce* (NY: 1958), 147n
Translation of Horace's 'O fons Bandusiæ'
  Gorman, *James Joyce: A Definitive Life* (London: 1941), 45–46
Translation of Verlaine's 'Chanson d'automne'
  Gorman, 59
On Rudolf Goldschmidt
  Gorman, 246–47
Fragment on Miss Moschos
  Colum, 121
Hue's Hue? or Dalton's Dilemma
  Spielberg, *James Joyce's Manuscripts and Letters at the University of Buffalo: A Catalogue* (Buffalo, NY: 1962), No. IV. B.7
Epigram on the Lady Friends of St James
  Colum, *Life and the Dream* (NY: 1947), 395
Pour la rîme seulement
  Spielberg, No. IV. B.13
Epilogue to Ibsen's *Ghosts*
  Gorman, 224–25
Translation from Gottfried Keller's *Lebendig Begraben* Suite
  Gorman, 342
A Come-All-Ye, by a Thanksgiving Turkey
  Joyce Memorial Committee. *Pastimes of James Joyce*, 1941
John Quinn
  Gorman, 247
Claude Sykes
  Gorman, 247
Solomon (on Simeone Levi)
  Gorman, 247

D.L.G.

    Gorman, 247

P. J. T.

    Spielberg, No. IV. B. 3

The Holy Office

    First circulated in Pola 1904–05

Gas from a Burner

    Printed in Trieste and circulated in Dublin during Joyce's lifetime

Ecce Puer

    Published in the *New Republic* (NY), LXXIII:939 (30.11.1932)

Index of Titles

Index of First Lines